The Road to Spiritual Success

A Journey to Becoming

A Collaborative Nonfiction by: Deion S. Pierre Sr., Tia Bernice, Abraham O. Sculley, Evencia Janvier, Jazmin Kylene, Lerone Gray, and Timone Brown

ISBN 978-0-578-78682-7

Editing and Book design by Chantel Gardner
Instagram: @LyfeWorks
Email: lyfeworksmvp@gmail.com

Visit and Connect with me here:
Instagram: @King.Deion44 @DreamTeam_TheLegacy
Email: KingDeion@dreamersjourney.live
Website: DreamersJourney.live
Text: 305-424-2632

This book is a roadmap for the individual who wakes up knowing that there is more to life than their current situation and wants to become better than they were yesterday but needs guidance.

Acknowledgements

I am extremely thankful to everyone who has served a purpose in my journey of becoming, your support has allowed me to publish my first book.

I would like to thank my creator first and foremost for this journey in itself and for allowing me to share the lessons I have learned with others.

Leonie Nelfrard, my aunt, I thank you for being my first spiritual guide. You answered every question I had pertaining to religion and spirituality, and you are the epitome of a faith-driven spiritual life. I love you Aunty.

Elvita Jeune, my grandma, I thank you for every prayer that you have placed over my life publicly and privately. You have impacted my spiritual life so much. I love you, Grandma.

Youseline Murat and Jonel Pierre, my mom and dad, I literally would not be here without you two. As young parents and kids to immigrants, you both have set a foundation, a foundation that was made to be built upon. You both have exemplified resiliency in ways that cannot be explained in a paragraph alone. You taught me to never give up and that I can always be better; that will stick with me for the rest of my life. I love you, Ma. I love you, Daddy.

Thank you to my siblings Eric, Isaiah, Paigge, Eathan, and Janelle for the continual push to be my best self. You all are the reason I have strived to be better every day (since as far back as I can remember), doing my best to set an example so that you can do even better. I love you all.

Tia Bernice, my co-author, business partner, and my Angel. I thank you for being my peace when my world seems chaotic. I thank you for your patience in my time of growth, and for educating me on the real meaning of gratitude, patience, and love. This book couldn't have been written without your love in my life. I love you, Angel.

Abraham Sculley, my right hand, my spiritual brother, and my son's Godfather, ever since the second grade you have been there as an open ear. You are always a call away if I ever need any guidance, in any way. My journey through spirituality would not be the same without your presence in my life. I am grateful for partnering with you in this book, love you brother.

Evencia Janvier, a great friend I hold dear, you have always been my definition of resiliency. The way that you have handled the trials and tribulations on your journey of becoming has influenced my life in so many ways. I thank you for all the love and long talks about growth and life, and I am glad to have you writing in this book. Love you Evey.

Jazmin Kylene, dear friend, and my son's Godmother, it is a pleasure having you write in this book. I have learned so much from you in the time I have been blessed to know you. You are the definition of manifesting greatness, everything you set out to do you are conquering and I will always admire that about you. You are the best Godmother my son could have. Thank you for being a part of this book Jaz, love you.

Timone Brown, a great friend, our long talks after workout sessions will always leave an impact on my life because you challenged me to open my perspective. The way you give back to the youth, helping them break the limitations life has placed on them is inspirational. You never allow me to settle and that is why

I will always appreciate our relationship and I'm very thankful for you being a part of this book, love you, T.
Lerone "Roc" Gray, I am so thankful for you being a part of this book. Your knowledge of health is impeccable. As my coach you have pushed me to go hard every day, not accepting anything less. I truly am thankful to be in your presence watching you achieve greatness daily, love you brother.

Last but certainly not least, Deion S. Pierre Jr., Deuce, my son. Deuce you are the reason why I wake up every day with the fuel to take on whatever life brings to me. I never thought the blessing of being your father would have impacted my life so much. I love you with every inch, organ, and breath in me. Although I know everyone's shoes take them on their own path in life, my hope is to grow through as many obstacles life has to offer so that I can guide you through them when the time comes. I love you Son.

Contents

Introduction

In life, there are many obstacles on our path to becoming the person that we were born to be. The situations and circumstances that get in the way of our growth can lead us into a life of turmoil, regrets, and unhappiness if we let them. Whether it's your finances, what is happening in the news, the status of our relationships (or lack thereof), etc. Unfortunately, we sometimes believe that the poor outcomes in these areas of life are "just the way life is." Well, it is not. Although life may not be all peaches and cream, it definitely does not have to be hell on earth either. In one of her famous songs, Hannah Montana said, "Life's what you make it, so let's make it rock!" I am a true believer in this affirmation. You are more than capable of altering your life and becoming the rockstar in the life of your choosing.

You might be asking yourself, how does one become a rock star in their own life? The first step would be to analyze your life right where you are now and to accept it. Accept where you are and also accept, with total belief, that wherever you are now is where you will no longer be. The journey to becoming is a daily process; it is becoming a better you than you were the day before.

It is the art of knowing better, so you begin to do better, but the results are not for anyone but yourself. Only you can enjoy the internal satisfaction of your becoming, and we all have the potential to become ANYTHING we choose. The journey has tests and challenges, but as long as you do not give up, the tests will turn into testimonies and the challenges into opportunities! Many may feel as if they already understand this, but there is a common misconception. Most people are looking for the "what" instead of the "who"; there is a big difference between the two areas of motivation.

What vs. Who

The "what" is when you were a kid being asked, "What do you want to become when you grow up?" Then you would give an answer such as a doctor, a lawyer, a judge, or a professional athlete. These are all great answers, but they are all found outside of yourself; all are external material wants. What you will do does not answer the question of who you will become?

The "who" is your being, your character, your attitude. When you become that doctor, who are you? Are you a happy doctor, or are you an impatient one? Are you a lawyer of optimism, or one of pessimism? Are you an athlete that puts forth the effort, or are you lazy? You can't find the answers to these questions outside of yourself. The 14th Dalai Lama said that "when you learn everything springs only from yourself, you will learn both peace and joy." Life begins to get much better when you learn to focus on bettering yourself from the inside out.

Your Guide

In life, whether you know it or not, most profoundly successful people have coaches. A coach's purpose is to help guide you on your journey of becoming. It may seem enticing to want to do it all by yourself. In current times you hear many stating that they are "self-made," but if you observe closely, they too have received assistance in some way, shape, or form. A successful musician would not be where they are without the DJ, producer, and promotion team that has helped them on their journey. Even if the musician has all the talent in the world, it is their team's assistance that helped put them in the position they are in.

If you look into the lives of some of the greatest, from Beyonce to Warren Buffet, you will see a coach, mentor, or guide of some sort. Guides do not only come in the form of an actual person you have met in real life, nowadays with the way technology has expanded, one can find a guide in their favorite social media influencers on various social platforms. But even with the advancements of modern technology, reading is still one of the best ways to receive life-changing assistance to better yourself.

Reading is essential to expanding your mind. It opens your brain past the complexities of your current situations. There are times when, due to life, you may feel trapped and in need of something that can give you hope. You may not have that guide, you may not even have the internet to use to your advantage, and that's ok. You can always go to your local library and check out a book that will spark a fire in you to take action on that very thing you always wanted to. Depending on the genre, books have the ability to broaden your perspective. Suppose you have a goal to learn how to manage your finances. You can read a book about that topic (financial literacy) that gives you the exact answer you have needed to move forward; thus guiding you toward your financial goals.

The Road to Spiritual Success is that guide for you! Although this is not the end all be all (with the perspective of various authors), our goal is to help you discover yourself beyond any limitation (whatever the reason or cause), and hold your hand through the process of spiritual transmutation.

Spiritual Keys

Throughout the book, you will find sectioned off exercises that are marked by keys. These exercises were thoughtfully crafted with your personal and spiritual development in mind. Growth is an interactive process, so each activity is meant to reinforce the skills and principles introduced. We encourage you to really delve beneath the surface and invest well thought out responses for the best results.

Study and Apply

While on your road to spiritual success, one must emphasize and continue to remember that it is the ROAD to spiritual success and not the rest stop at spiritual success. The word road is defined in Middle English as "a riding, or a journey." With this being said, just as you have your whole life of education where you studied to learn a new skill, you must also study this text. It is said that we only retain 10 percent of the books we read, so utilize this text over and over. All of the information in this text has been collectively amassed through years of experience; it will not suffice to only read once and throw it to the side. Study, study, study! Studying is the devotion of time given to acquiring knowledge.

Keep in mind that there is no use in studying if you will not apply what you learned. I assume we have all heard the cliche that knowledge is power. I want to challenge that statement with the following information: knowledge does not become power until it is applied. Think about some of the greats, Oprah Winfrey, Kobe Bryant, Beyonce, etc... if they had only acquired the skill of their respective fields and not applied them, would we still label them as greats? The answer is no.

Practice creates progression. It's not hard, it's not easy, it's simple; you just have to take it. Take *The Road to Spiritual Success.*

Chapter 1

Love Your Neighbor As Yourself

Romans 13:9 "...Love your neighbor as yourself."

In In this day and age, loving is an action most are scared of, yet it is one of our deepest desires. Throughout the ages of time, the meaning of the word love has been misconstrued and watered down. Without any real knowledge behind the word, we often look for it in a state of *ignorance*– the lack of knowledge or information. In life, we, myself included, have been taught and conditioned –through the paths and connections that information is brought to us through, whether it be our family or the television- to seek an emotion or a feeling, disguised as the word love, externally.

When I say seek love externally, I mean to look somewhere outside of ourselves to receive and obtain it. Through many first and second-hand life experiences, I have studied the word love and its true meaning; I learned that it's often sought out of misconceptions. As humans, we are blessed with the ability to think and reason, but most will throw out logic when it comes to our emotional needs for love. Because of the desire that we naturally have to experience love (whether it's due to the feelings of loneliness, or the longing for happiness, etc.), it can influence us to think with our hearts before thinking with our minds, causing us to lose ourselves.

In this chapter, I will debunk the way you look at love and add a new meaning of the word to your life; a meaning that will not only spark the desire of it, but how you can receive it as well. As I said at the beginning of the chapter, love (for most) is being sought somewhere outside of ourselves: in relationships, material items, and money. Although all these things are wonderful and nice, they can never truly fill the void of real love. Love is intended to be found inwardly, not outwardly.

"Love your neighbor as yourself." This is such a powerful statement by the apostle Paul. Let's break down this statement. Even though Paul states that you must love your neighbor, he goes on to say as yourself. This is the first step to love yourself. Once this truth has resonated and been established with new ways of thinking, the first half of the statement will have no choice but to happen instinctively.

In order to love yourself, you have to know exactly what love is. Not by your own definition, but by its true definition. When thinking about love, what is the first thing that comes to mind? Love is commercially defined as the affection for a person, place, or thing; whether that be family, your romantic partner, or your favorite meal at a restaurant. Everything I have mentioned is outside of yourself. This reminds me of a line in a song which states, "Looking for love in all the wrong places." You might be saying to yourself that there is nothing wrong with that; you might actually feel very comfortable doing this very thing. The problem with that is that all of those things can go away, not to say indefinitely, but the truth is people and relationships die, and restaurants close. When and if they do you will still feel empty because you are trying to find love without rather within.

When I became aware of this, my first question was, "What does love truly mean? And how do I fill this void on the inside?" I was blessed to come across a new meaning in the word "love" through my curiosity. After scrolling past about nine or ten different definitions, I finally found one that changed the form of the word from a noun to a verb. This was shocking to me. I had always known love to be a verb, but yet still applied it by its definition as a noun. The new definition states to cherish, but since I had not known the definition of love to begin with, I thought that I should probably look up what it meant to cherish. The etymology, or origin of the word cherish means "to encourage in the mind". And encourage means to give support, confidence, or to make strong. So to 'love yourself' means to make yourself strong, to support yourself, and to give yourself confidence. Wow! Read that again. Love is a state of being.

Take a minute to pause and just think about how often you truly support yourself and make YOU confident without others help or support. How often do you look in the mirror and tell yourself that you are beautiful or handsome? How often do you tell yourself you are great and blessed? Do you talk yourself down, or do you lift yourself up? Do you truly love yourself? Evaluate this honestly.

After your evaluation, if you find that you do not love yourself as much as you'd like to, don't judge yourself. Judging yourself will only continue to tear you down and not aid in uplifting you. Instead, use your newfound awareness to shift the tide in your life. Love is infinite. Make it your business to love yourself every day. When you look into the mirror, create yourself a new truth. Tell yourself "I can do all things and be great at, I look amazing, and all things are working for my good". No matter how you may feel, you must encourage yourself; you must love yourself.

Love Yourself as your Neighbor was strategically placed as the first chapter for a reason. You are your home and love is the brick you have to lay to make the foundation of your home, you, strong. To not love yourself is to build a home with a weak foundation, causing your home, you, to eventually collapse. Remember, laying the foundation is only the beginning; there is much more to building a home, so keep reading.

Chapter 2

The Power of Stillness

In search of combatting depression or anxiety, many of us venture out on a life-long quest to find joy. But oftentimes, the joy we eventually do capture seems to be fleeting and slip right through our fingers because it wasn't what we were meant to be chasing in the first place. The peace we crave is achieved when we choose to embrace stillness and presence, sitting with the range of emotions that we're blessed to feel instead of trying to cloak them in happiness. This chapter will explore why we've been conditioned into thinking that fast-paced living means we're more valuable, why it's important to remember our true purpose, and reconnect with the beings that we are beneath our fears and egos by embracing stillness.

Some of the methodology we explore in this search for stillness derives from different ancient practices and religions, ranging from Hinduism to Tai Chi. Humankind has long embarked on a path of self-discovery, documenting it in scriptures and garnering the tools necessary to harness peace. Though it's become more challenging to attain with the rise of capitalism and social media, we can rest assured that the framework these belief systems have provided us remains effective. Mindfulness as a practice is a nonjudgmental state of complete awareness. Committing to this awareness of one's thoughts, emotions, or experiences, is a commitment we have struggled to make for centuries, yet affirm is the answer to finding our what and our why. These ancient practices teach us how to honor life's fundamental and existential questions, not by searching for it outside ourselves, but rather quieting our minds and going within.

Stillness is something that is highly sought after, yet seemingly unattainable within the human experience. It doesn't matter what part of the world you live in; there isn't an ounce of doubt that you can, to some extent, agree with the statement: we live in a "microwave" culture. Everything has to get done fast. It's like there's an imaginary stopwatch planted in our heads, always having us on alert for a deadline that truly doesn't exist!

When we're in middle school, we're panicking over high school. When we're in high school, we're panicking over college. When we're in college, we're panicking over joining the workforce. Once we begin our careers, we're panicking over settling down and starting a family. Then it's parenthood and retirement, and the next inevitable obstacle society somehow placed onto your path.

Life is meant to be a stroll, and yet we've made it into a relay race. We've lost sight of the value in doing things just out of sheer amusement because we are so invested in the ideal of productivity. If we're not creating, gaining, networking, making money, or just flat out working, we don't see ourselves as valuable. Stillness challenges us to pause and mute the noise for a bit and allow ourselves to be at rest within our bodies, to feel the earth beneath us and connect to the rhythm of our breath. Stillness reintroduces us to what it means to be human, which has far less to do with productivity and much more to do with simply being.

Our missions are complete once we accept that we don't have to DO or MAKE something to validate our personal value! Our value comes from the energy we emit, the love we pour out into the world, the divine, karmic role we play. (No matter what higher Source you believe in,) I'm sure you don't believe that you were created for the sole purpose of making money, feeding capitalism, and working a 9 to 5.

Our passions, careers, and daily affairs are beautiful and essential, especially if they bring us joy. Whether you're an entrepreneur, a healer, a teacher, a retail worker, an athlete, or an artist, there is nothing shameful about dedicating yourself to a craft you love and making money from it. But nine times out of ten, these roles won't provide you with the lasting fulfillment we all seem to crave. They are the sprinkles on top of a good life, but they aren't our reason or our purpose; our why is much bigger than the titles our careers gift us.

Stillness

Our reason is found when we attain stillness. When we are able to be centered, quiet our egos, and feel our own bodies, we can really hear our souls and step into the best possible version of ourselves.

The peace that you cultivate when you dedicate yourself to stillness will trickle into the parts of your life that actually aren't still at all. The more you seek stillness, the more you'll have access to peace, whether you lead an overstimulating life or not. You'll find that triggers that used to push you over the edge don't even have the power to upset you anymore. You'll be a more attentive friend, partner, and human, mastering the art of conversation because listening and being present suddenly come as second nature. You'll present a better-quality version of yourself to the world simply by being more "here."

While it seems like something so far away, stillness is always within our reach, whether we choose to grab it or not. Don't believe me? Exercise reading this paragraph, take a moment to put this book down and close your eyes. Give yourself a couple of deep breaths, fully inhaling and fully exhaling. Notice the chair you're sitting in or the bed you're lying on. Feel their texture, the foundation of earth supporting you. Take a moment to hear all the sounds of your environment, near and far. Maybe cars are passing outside of your window or a dishwasher rumbling just outside your door. Honor every noise, big and small. Allow yourself to feel all of the sensations in your body, from head to toe. Are you holding tension in your jaw, your forehead? Is there a heaviness elsewhere in your body that you hadn't noticed? Loosen up and just be. Really just be. This is stillness; this is what being "here" feels like.

Presence

Being "here" truly is our superpower. It can only be done when we are in the present moment, yet so much of our collective suffering stems from our inability to stay within it. As humans, we can easily stray from where our physical body is and let our minds wander to places that frankly don't exist. While it may feel just as electric in our emotional currents, the past only truly exists within our memories. And our future, while it may serve as our drive and willingness, only exists within our imagination. All that we have is the present, the gift of now. It's up to us whether or not we choose to exist within it.

When we mentally exist in the future, we are actively choosing to miss out on our lives. If we can't wait to get to a place where we'll achieve something and "finally be happy," we won't notice the smells, sensations, or tiny details that make life special. This is where expectation takes over, and the fears, anxieties, and doubts begin the trickle in.

When we mentally exist in the past, we are also actively choosing to miss out on our lives! When we focus on what could have been or rework scenarios to play out the way we would have preferred them to, we miss the reason why things even played out the way they did in the first place. Everything happens for a reason, and if you would root yourself in that belief, you'd understand that reality couldn't have gone any other way. Every decision, mistake, and risk led you to exactly where you are now, and where you are now is exactly where you're meant to be.

In the present, we have our eureka moments and life-changing revelations. It's when the most divinely guided ideas plop themselves into our heads. That's because in stillness, we connect to our core (our core being the centered part of us that isn't led by anxiety or fear), and all of the ego-driven thoughts holding us back suddenly don't have the microphone. It's when our higher selves can finally get a word in! Mother Teresa once said, "Before you speak, it is necessary for you to listen, for God speaks in the silence of the heart." Present stillness empowers us by giving us enough silence to hear ourselves finally.

Methods

There are plenty of ways to help ease your mind without working yourself into mental overdrive with thoughts of where you need to be, or mistakes you shouldn't have made, and so on and so forth. Here are some breakdowns of methods you can try; many of them require mental agility, while others are physical. I invite you to incorporate whichever resonates with you into a regular practice.

It's important to keep in mind that none of these practices are more effective than the other; it's all just a matter of what works for you! You can even incorporate more than one and let yourself be intuitively led. There's truly no right or wrong here. Each of these exercises shares the common thread of putting you in the present moment and allowing your mind to go on autopilot mode.

To master stillness to the best of your ability, you must commit to it. It should be a part of your spiritual practice. Maintaining your spiritual hygiene is quite similar to maintaining your physical hygiene. You can't shower once and expect to be clean forever, just like you can't meditate once and expect to maintain peace for the rest of your life. There are commitment and consistency required, a mental muscle you continuously need to work to strengthen. But just like with weightlifting, the 10-pound dumbbells feel lighter and lighter the more you use them, and pretty soon, you'll need at least 20 pounds if you want to feel a challenge.

And lastly, don't judge yourself! Cultivating kind inner dialogue is crucial to your spiritual journey in general. If you become critical of yourself for veering off alignment or getting easily distracted by thoughts, then congratulations–, you're human! There's no need to punish yourself; even the most advanced of gurus experience the exact same thing. We're not seeking perfection; we're seeking intention. Set the intention to find peace within stillness, and it will find you, bit by bit.

•Breath-work

Connecting to our breath is the quickest and most effective way to tap into the present moment and regain control over our minds. Just taking a few mindful breaths in, filling up your lungs entirely, and slowly letting go can be enough to plug you in. Dr. Richard Brown, an associate clinical professor of psychiatry at Columbia University and co-author of The Healing Power of the Breath, has noted that "controlled breathing can change the body's autonomic response of the nervous system, which controls many unconscious processes." Challenge yourself to connect with your breath more often, in moments of meditation and the periods in between.

- **Meditation**

It's well understood that meditation practically hands over the gift of peace on a platter in exchange for your stillness. Whether your meditations are guided or silent, five minutes or fifty, it's one of the most critical practices for anyone seeking to strengthen their inner spiritual power. It's intimidating to approach meditation when you're looking from the outside-in. I understand that quieting your thoughts can seem like an impossible feat. But the goal isn't necessarily to stop thinking; it's to stop engaging with your thinking. Play the part of an observer and let whatever plants itself into your mind dissipate just as quickly as it came.

- **Prayer**

No matter what your faith or spirituality looks like, praying is a very powerful way to ground you in the present moment as well. It allows your mind to go on autopilot while you experience life solely through your heart. This process not only anchors you into stillness, but it also strengthens your relationship with the universe! The author of The Healing Path of Prayer, Ron Roth, shares in the final chapter of his novel, "it's better to pray for ten minutes a day, every day of the week than to sit for two or three hours every once in a while." There's no blueprint, as long as you take the one-on-one time with your Source as seriously as you would reconnecting with an old friend.

- **Nature**

There's no other way of saying it; nature is truly the closest we can genuinely get to raw, untouched purity. Simply going for a walk on a nature trail or riding your bike around your neighborhood is enough to connect you with your human core and drop you into the present moment. Taking along some high-vibe music with you is totally okay, but I invite you to spend some time listening and detailing the ambient sounds of what outside has to offer. Birds singing, wind whistling, and every other component can help you appreciate the now. Take in all the colors, sounds, and sensations.

- **Movement**

If you're a person who is uncomfortable with the idea of physically sitting still, then you're certainly in the majority. Luckily, there are many ways to find stillness inwardly while moving outwardly! Mindful movement can come in many, many forms. Even playing your favorite sport can connect you to stillness; repetitive motion invites your mind to go into autopilot mode and exist within the present moment. The most commonly enjoyed moving meditation would be yoga, which is the intersection between breath and movement, wholly rooted in keeping the mind still and present.

My Practice

As stated before, stillness is a mental muscle that you have to consistently work at strengthening, most ideally with a committed spiritual practice. There's no right or wrong as far as what that practice looks like; it can be any of the methods we discussed or even a combination. You'll always intuitively know what your mind and body need in that given instance!

As far as my personal practice goes, I always do my best to keep it within the first half-hour of waking. It feels easier for me to quiet my mind on an empty stomach, preferably before I've been overstimulated by checking texts and social media (though that's definitely something I have to work at keeping consistent). I have a sacred space at home decorated and equipped with all the tools I need to feel my most connected. This includes my crystals, vision board, rosary and prayer beads, candles, a prayer rug, and sage, but all you really need is your intention. I keep the space clean physically and energetically, never using it for anything other than meditation and prayer. I usually start with a few deep breaths, a still meditation, and oftentimes end with prayer, or just an honest talk with the universe. I choose to make my practice extra-long on Tuesdays because I find that having a dedicated day makes it easier to commit to.

This is what strengthening my access to peace looks like for me, and the results definitely trickle into who I am in my waking day-to-day. I don't react to situations that would have otherwise invoked anxiety or anger easily, and I'm able to notice the smaller details of life that make it so beautiful. But this is not a one size fits all routine!

While exerting all of this extra effort into making my meditation space as sacred as possible definitely helps to elevate my vibration and make the transition easier, I can also safely say that I feel just as close to my core when I walk through a nature trail, watch a sunset, or write a piece of poetry. It doesn't take a church pew, prayer rug, or any mystical tools to connect with your inner peace. It's all about your intentions to do so.

My morning ritual sets a powerful tone for the rest of my day and allows me to walk presently in each step. Renowned spiritual healer Ron Roth shares, "When eating, just eat. When walking, just walk. Be fully present in your simplest actions and do not overlay them with fantasy, fear, regret, or distraction." It is actively choosing to be still in the gift of the moment that you're in where true happiness and connection to divinity happens.

Chapter 3

Gratitude is the Attitude

"Acknowledging the good that you already have in your life is the foundation for all abundance."

-Eckhart Tolle

Gratitude... a word that resonated with me so much, that in 2017 I got it tattooed on my forearm. A word that I knew needed to be with me at all times. Life is funny because after I had just left the tattoo shop, my cousin and I were driving down one of Richmond, VA's main roads. We approached a stoplight. To our right, we saw a huge, blue banner with the word GRATITUDE written in big, white letters, "randomly" hanging from a popular furniture store named; Haverty's. If you know me, you know I use the word "randomly" very seldom as I do not believe in coincidences., Although I had driven past this store countless times, this banner that I had never seen before was divinely displayed for me to see. At that moment, I was provided validation from The Most High. Any doubt or regret I had after finally getting my first tattoo (without telling my parents and fearful that they'd condemn me) quickly vanished. Almost three years later, I now write this chapter understanding exactly why that incident was no coincidence.

For those who don't know, to express gratitude or to be

grateful means to express thankfulness. It means to proclaim your appreciation for anything in your life. If you look further into the etymology, or history, of the word "gratitude," you will also find that the roots of this word trace back to meaning: to praise, to celebrate, or to be in contact with the divine. For me, this deeper meaning adds so much more value to the word gratitude. It now can be interpreted to mean: to praise or give thanks to a higher, or even God-like, power. And if we were to go and look again at the etymology of the word gratitude, you will find that it mentions "the divine." The word "divine" simply implies a "god-like" figure.

The purpose of this chapter is not to persuade anyone into the direction of one specific god or the next. However, if you are reading this book, I am certain that you understand the idea or meaning of spirituality in some way. To be spiritual means that you understand that there is something greater than us; you feel or believe that there is a greater entity. To realize that there is SOMETHING greater than all of us is vital.

Above all else, I know that we are all one, all on The Road to Spiritual Success. All of us are persevering throughout life with one main goal, that is peace and happiness. I may not have the specific steps that you need to take to achieve that goal however, what I do know for certain is that the power of gratitude is one that can transform, shift, and redefine your life indefinitely– leading you directly down the Road to Spiritual Success.

In addition to understanding the power of gratitude, one must understand the power of manifestation. The power of gratitude lies hand in hand with the power of manifestation or speaking things into existence. To begin, the root of the word manifestation is manifest; translation: to make public. Manifestation begins in your mind. It starts with your thoughts.

As you begin to embody and internalize thoughts, in turn, those thoughts externalize.

We've all heard the phrase, "as a man thinks, so is he. (Proverbs 23:7)" We all understand the power that our minds hold. Our minds control every aspect of our lives. Be it your conscious or subconscious thoughts, our dreams, overt/covert opinions, anxieties, worries, fears, etc... All stem from our thoughts. Our thoughts become true reflections of our realities, beliefs, insecurities, egos; you name it.

Being someone who once suffered from anxiety, I understand the influence of the mind and how your thoughts can affect your life daily. This ties into the power of gratitude because I had to change the way I thought and what I thought about to rid myself of my severe anxieties. Beforehand, I took for granted all that I had. I spent my nights stuck in my negative thinking; I even did my research on things that ultimately hurt me. I was convinced that something was wrong all the time, and that sent me down a path of self-destruction. I was not grateful for my health, peace of mind, happiness, etc.... and my thoughts lured me down a hole filled with restlessness and worry. Until one day, I realized I had to be still and focus my thoughts on the positive. I had to dissociate from my old patterns of thinking and not refer to myself as an "anxiety sufferer" while focusing my thoughts on what I was grateful for. Even while I was still considering myself to be an "anxious person".

Negativity is commonly referred to as a "dark cloud." However, a sky filled with dark clouds can not keep away the sun. No matter the amount or size of those clouds, the sun is always there waiting for its time to shine. I've had many days where my mind has felt foggy or cloudy; I lacked the motivation to do anything. My pessimistic thoughts remained a stubborn overcast that felt like it would never go away, and on days like that, I had to start small. I had to make a conscious effort to shift my thoughts to only focus on the good. I began by only focusing on the simple fact that there is life in me. "I am alive." "I am well." These were constant thoughts I had to repeat to myself daily.

"Think about what you are grateful for and express it."

The next step in this is the power of speaking all that you are grateful for. I learned how to improve progressively, I had to begin to proclaim and state aloud all that I have to be grateful for. I expressed thanks for the air in my lungs; there are many people gasping for their last. I expressed thanks for the sound of mowing lawns; there are people that are deaf. I expressed gratitude for the ability I have to see, because there are so many that are blind; both physically and spiritually. These two actions, both thinking and speaking all that I was grateful for, brought me out of a dark place. Without these two things, I can not imagine where my life would be today. Realizing all that I did have instead of dwelling on what was not even real/existent; allowed the sun to shine again in my life.

Together, let's think of the easiest thing you can do while you're reading this book RIGHT NOW. Everyone reading this, stop and simply look up. Shift your eyes from off of this page to have them land on whatever's above you. Be it a ceiling, the sky, the roof of your car, etc. All I've asked of you to do is to use the muscles in your eyes, and the ability that you possess to control your eyes and look up! Simple enough, right?

Now, to shift your perspective a little, I'll share with you the life of someone that I know personally and interact with very closely. This person is legally blind and experiences great discomfort doing exactly what you just did. With one prosthetic eye and the other eye having very limited muscular abilities, this person struggles daily and to do something as "simple" as looking up is quite a challenge. This very task that we all take for granted is one that I have learned to be grateful for. Controlling your thoughts, shifting your mindset, and empathizing with others are just a few tactics you can use to learn to become a more grateful person.

The more you think about what you are grateful for, the more said things appear. In addition to that, the more that you speak of happiness and appreciation for what you have, the more abundantly said things materialize as well. Power lies in your thoughts. Power lies within all that you speak. Once your thoughts and speech intertwine with gratitude, your life will transform in ways you never believed possible.

As I stated previously, you can have gratitude for ANYTHING. There is nothing too small or too insignificant that you can not find the beauty in and be grateful for. Change your perspectives and outlooks, get into the habit of being a more thankful person. Frequently think about what you are grateful for and express it. Once done, watch as you receive what your life has been missing.

How to begin allowing the power of gratitude to transform your life:

- First, gain control over your thoughts. We, as people, have thousands of thoughts per day. Remember, you are in control of your thoughts. Train your mind to think: positively, innovatively, kindly, upliftingly, peacefully, and happily.
- Then, remove comparative language from your vocabulary that motivates constant competition. For

example, words like: better, worst, easier, faster, etc. If you are using these words to put down yourself or the things you are blessed with, stop. If you are using these words to define who you are or your worth. STOP. Believe that you are enough. Be grateful for all that you are.

- Next, shift your narrative. The things you think, believe, and speak, ultimately manifest in your life. Be sure that you are only thinking, believing, and expressing gratitude. Mold the path that lies ahead by being grateful for what you have right now.

- Lastly, shift your perspective. Turn everything into something positive and find the goodness in what you possess. Refocus your energy on all that you have to be grateful for.

If you find that there isn't much to be grateful for around you, begin by putting yourself in someone else's shoes. In doing so, you will quickly find just how fortunate you are and how often people long for the very things that you're taking for granted. Relish in gratitude and watch your life evolve.

My challenge to you:

Throughout my journey of becoming an, overall, more grateful person, I've stumbled across individuals that also emphasize the importance and power of gratitude. Comedian, entertainer, entrepreneur, and mogul Steve Harvey often speaks on the power of gratitude throughout his life's journey. He says:

"Gratitude erases all negativity... it's not a magic trick. Joy and depression cannot reside in the same space. Gratitude changes your perception. Perception changes your existence."

This specific way of thinking is what can help anyone catapult their life into precisely what they want. Gratitude is the attitude, and when you begin to understand how your "perspective controls your reality" and "how habits tend to manifest," (both of which are topics in this book), the inevitable will occur.

I challenge all readers of this book to complete the same practice that Steve Harvey uses explained below:

Sit down with a journal, and designate it as your "gratitude journal." In it, write out all of which you possess that you are grateful for. With this exercise, I also challenge you to think about what you may not have always considered a "blessing" as well. Think about the things that you may at one point in time presumed to be "negative." Be sure to write out as much as possible.

One other aspect I want you to be mindful of while writing out your list is to write with intention. Before you begin to write each item, be sure to write (and truly possess) gratitude. Each sentence should start with:

"I am so grateful for..."

Write what you mean and mean what you write. Also, keep in mind that this could take a couple of days, as you should have quite a bit to be grateful for! Nonetheless, be sure to complete this practice and, when done, proceed to write a list of what you'd like to have. View this list as your "wants" or your "manifestations." When you write this list, don't simply write what you think would be nice or cool to have. Actually write out your desires, and when you write them, begin each sentence by writing:

"I am so happy and grateful NOW that I have..."

By doing this, you are not only speaking what you want into existence as if it is already yours, but you are now giving and expressing even more thanks/gratitude for what is already yours in the future. Understand the power that a practice like this truly holds.

As time goes on, be sure to continue to refer back to these lists. In due time you will notice that the once separate lists have now begun to come together as one. More and more items from your "desires" list will become a part of what you now possess. Because you chose to focus on what you are grateful for, you wrote down your desires and gave thanks for what you have (and will have), your desires will be manifested into your life.

Always keep this quote in mind by Oprah Winfrey when thinking about gratitude:

"If you concentrate on what you have, you will always end up having more. Even if it's just $2. If you focus on what you don't have, you will never ever have enough."

Remember: gratitude + belief = your new reality.

Chapter 4

Health is Wealth

"You cannot enjoy wealth if you're not in good health"

-Anonymous

"Happiness is the highest form of health"

-Dalai Lama

Hello Kings and Queens, I would first like to introduce myself formally. My name is Coach Roc Gray, and I am the owner of Go Hard Performance Systems; a brand focused on helping individuals "Grow in Greatness" through a holistic approach to strength and performance training. Now, let us be honest here, how often do you hear the phrase "Health is wealth" but never get a real explanation of what it means? I would imagine that you would be filthy rich if you invested in this whole health thing for all the times you have heard this. Well, my question to you is, why haven't you? "Health is wealth" is the overall understanding that your being is a walking investment. So why wouldn't you invest in the richest resource you have, your health? Maybe I can help you understand how to maximize your internal wealth so that it may show more vividly externally.

Take this into consideration: For those who play sports, especially at a high level, the number one thing coaches talk about is a person's ability. Let us be honest here. It is the main reason that person is in a given position of opportunity. I will give you a few names, and you tell me what stands out about them the most: Michael Jordan, Deion Sanders, LeBron James, Mike Trout, and Kobe Bryant. Is there anything (aside from them being extremely gifted athletes and people) that stands out to you about these individuals? Do you know what's the most remarkable ability in sports that they all have in common? Availability!

Let me break this down for you. Say you are an individual who works from 9 A.M. to 5 P.M., Monday through Friday, and you get paid $100 per hour. Now consider your total earnings if you are available to work those hours each day with no problem. Now, with that same figure in mind, imagine the amount of money you would earn if you only worked half of those hours. This little analogy is illustrating the state of your health in a good place compared to it being in a bad place. No matter how amazing they are, all the individuals I listed have all had this one distinct factor in common that propelled them from "good" athletes to being "great" athletes! All of them have invested significantly in their health, thus allowing them to be available on a consistent basis. They knew that in order to showcase their talents, their health was of the highest priority. And because of that consistent effort, their material wealth has exceeded anything they could have ever imagined. Each person listed has missed maybe 15% of the games they played in their entire careers. Compare that to individuals like Bo Jackson or Percy Harvin, who were phenomenally gifted but did not have huge careers due to not being available in their sport. If you are healthy and accessible, you are able to receive more.

Your health is not just how you look, but it is how you feel. Society teaches us that to be happy, we must have a six-pack, eat salads, and live in the gym. What if I told you that was false? Now, don't get me wrong; eating junk food all the time and being inactive does nothing good for you (mentally or physically). Still, there are levels to where health and happiness meet for everyone. It is intersectional. For example, if you are diligent about working out or being active, 2-4x's a week, who is to say (barring any serious or chronic health issues) that you can't enjoy a cookie on the weekends? Many of us chase a specific goal or lifestyle blindly and lose connection with how we feel while doing it. TRUE optimal health comes from doing something good for your body that you can enjoy!

Two years ago, I had a client who we will call Aisha (which just so happens to mean living prosperous, a.k.a. wealth in Arabic and Swahili). Aisha weighed 185 pounds when I met her and was incredibly determined to weigh 150 pounds again (what she weighed in high school). She felt that she would be happier at that weight, and I gave her my word that I would help, but I also told her to "consider how you feel as we get close to that number. You may decide along the way that it isn't the focal point anymore." Although she heard me, her mind was still set on weighing 150 pounds, so down in weight we went. At 180 pounds, she started to notice her back and core felt stronger, at 175 pounds she was excited that her old clothes didn't fit anymore, and she went shopping. It was when she weighed 170 pounds, something interesting happened.

Aisha told me that she felt more confident, that she received so many compliments, and she felt the best combination of strength and happiness at that weight than ever before. She said, "I think I am good right here," in an almost relieved tone. "I literally have the best of both worlds; I am fit and happy. I am able to eat pizza without feeling guilty, but also feel amazing in my own skin." Although she was incredibly determined to get to a certain number, she realized that what she felt was more important than what she thought her goal needed to be. That, my friends, is what true health looks like. It is the ability to be in-tune with your thoughts, feelings, and how those affect you positively. That is why your health literally is wealth! It is from a wealth of healthy emotions and thoughts that lead to opportunities you could not even imagine.

Let me ask you something; humor me if you will. Can you take a moment and think about something that brings you the most joyful and warm feeling? What are you doing at that moment? How about this, if you could look into the future, what do you see yourself doing that brings you happiness? I can almost bet that the moments you remembered or envisioned dealt with some form of activity, where you physically DID something. If my assumptions are correct, then I dare you to consider that feeling from that thought and manifest that into your everyday life. Let it motivate you. If it was a future thought, consider what it would take to make that happen. I'm more than sure that it will require you to be healthy and active to enjoy it fully.

If you asked me how to create good feelings that match the ones you've envisioned, I would say finding an activity that promotes good health and peace. If it aids in your happiness, it is a good start. Now, this activity will not look the same for everybody. For instance, I love to lift weights, play sports, and hike. Each of these activities helps me in different aspects of my life. Lifting weights forces me to let go of the emotions I may be holding onto and relieve stress. Playing sports brings me joy and gives me excitement in my everyday life. Taking a hike helps me engage in stress-free, peaceful thinking. All three of these activities bring about the same goal but in different ways. So, I would strongly advise you to figure out what activities bring you peace of mind while also improving your health and invest as much time as you can into it. If you were to commit to doing so for at least 90 days (three months), your life and the course you are on would drastically change for the better. Always remember this: anything that brings you sadness, or takes away from your happiness, or makes your health decline is not something you should invest energy into.

Your health thrives from experiences that promote peace, joy, and a strong sense of self-worth.

Don't believe me? Well, let me tell you a story.

At the time of writing this, I am 28 years old and extremely healthy overall. My mental state is great, my physical health is the best it has been in the past few years, and more importantly, I am genuinely happy in life. Do you want to know what the biggest contribution to my current healthy state in life is? It is that I am invested in my health more than I have ever been in my life! When I was in college, football was LIFE! My days consisted of sleeping, eating, breathing, and moving solely for football. There was not a moment in the day where football was not the main or only thing on my mind. I would stay up late at night thinking about playing professional football, go to sleep and dream about it, then wake up the next morning and go work towards it. I simply did things because I heard that it would make me a better football player. So even when I did not feel like it, even when I desired to do other things that made me happy, I focused on football. That consisted of working out 2-3 times a day, eating close to 6,000 calories a day, and even cutting off time with loved ones just so I could focus on football.

If you have not caught on yet, I was not happy in the midst of all of this, and truthfully, I wasn't that healthy either. I dealt with a lot of migraines and injuries simply because I didn't give my body time to rest, and trust me when I tell you, I paid for it! But how? How could using every waking moment of my life to work towards my dreams be a negative thing? Let me explain it further to you. When you commit every thought and action towards a goal, something will be sacrificed. Everyone around me told me to grind, go hard, to work relentlessly, which makes sense, but the missing key was proper balance. I did not have to run myself into the ground. All of those nights when I stayed up grinding, I should have been sleeping because recovery is important for physical AND mental health. This sleep deprivation led to migraines which led to missed classes, practices and moments that I could never get back. Another effect of less rest and recovery meant that my body didn't properly heal.I experienced chronic hamstring strains. These injuries are part of the reason I didn't have the athletic career that I dreamed of.

Due to me transferring schools and the process behind it, I missed out on the opportunity to play football in my senior year. Because of this I wasn't a prime candidate for the NFL anymore, but I kept that same vigor and determination to make my dreams come true. I tried out for the CFL, the baby brother of the NFL, and again, I didn't prioritize my health. Ultimately, I didn't make it even though I had sacrificed so much. Crushed and hurt (mentally and emotionally), I fell into a state of depression, which troubled me for about two years. Have you ever heard the statement, "where the mind goes, the body will follow?" Well, let me save you some trouble and tell you that it is absolutely true! Without football I lost purpose, I lost the reason to get up and work hard every day. I lost the thing that I thought made me the happiest and, in a sense, the thing that kept my physical health on a high. So, for the next couple of years, as I searched to find what truly made me happy, I allowed my overall health to fall by the wayside. This showed up in the forms of restless nights, poor eating, a lack of activity/exercise, and overall, I just lacked joy. All of the time I invested into my football career had caused my health to decline and ultimately put me in a position where I had to make a hard decision. I had to decide whether football or my health mattered more.

Following this conversation I had with myself, I put some things into perspective. The first thing I had to realize was that football didn't MAKE me happy, but it AIDED my happiness. There were plenty of other things that contributed to my overall happiness, and I needed to invest time into those things to reconstruct my health. Secondly, I realized that food is fuel, and I needed to treat it as such. Our bodies react well to a balance of nutrients from various sources. There is nothing wrong with eating super healthy, but do it because you will enjoy it while your body thanks you for it. I no longer eat every 2 hours like a robot but have a well-balanced nutrition plan that consists of the foods I need and foods that I love.

Lastly, I realized that I had explicitly trained my body for the purpose of football and football only. I wanted to make sure that I looked the part physically as well as performed on the field. It was always "make sure I have a six pack," and it definitely came at a cost. Now, although I am in great shape, I do not concern myself with whether I have chiseled abs or not. If they are there, then great, but if not, I'm ok with that too! I'm not focused solely on how my body looks, but how my body feels. And let me tell you, my muscles and joints have not felt this good in a LONG time. I feel fast, strong, agile, and most importantly, healthy! My focus is on my overall well-being; I'm making sure that my physical, mental, spiritual, and emotional health are balanced and equally invested in. Health is much more than how you look or what people think of you. Your health is how you feel, how you move, and how you enjoy life –balancing these components is where the understanding that "health is wealth" flourishes. It doesn't matter if you are an aspiring professional athlete, a stay-at-home mom of 4, or a fitness enthusiast. Please understand that your wellness is the most significant investment that you will ever make.

Think of a car that you keep driving until the oil runs empty. Eventually, the engine and car will perform worse and worse until it breaks down for good. That is our body! These lessons are what drive me to teach my clients balance, proper recovery, and more importantly, that they are humans, not machines. This knowledge alone, allows them to live happily, but more importantly, it places a higher value on their wholeness because when it comes to wellness, no one facet of health will function highly without the others. Your health and the wealth found in that will take you places you could never imagine. So go get active, go be enriched, and go **"Grow in Greatness!"**

Chapter 5

Habits Tend To Manifest

"Insanity is doing the same thing over and over again and expecting different results."
-Albert Einstein

What makes you stay committed to the things that are not bringing you closer to what you want? The answer is... HABITS.

I used to get the side-eye a lot from leaving the toilet seat up. My wife would say the same thing each time, "Babe can you stop leaving the toilet seat up?" And each time, I would apologize and actually be sincere in my apology, but for some reason, it was like I was in a trance whenever I went to use the toilet.

Truthfully, I was in a "trance-like" state. For years, I lived by myself with my own bathroom and no one to share it with. It was common practice for me to put the seat up when I went to use the toilet and not worry about ever putting it back down until I needed to take care of serious business. I had trained my brain to respond in a specific way when I went to use the bathroom, and after days, months, and years of training, I no longer had to think about what I did. Through training, I developed a habit.

The dictionary defines a habit as "a settled tendency or usual manner of behavior." Habits are powerful, and they ultimately create who you are, but understand that you have complete control over your them. Once you accept the responsibility of shaping and modifying your habits, then you will find that you can manifest anything into your life.

First, it's important to recognize that habits are neither good nor bad; they are just habits. However, your habits are significant pieces to your life's puzzle. They will either take you closer to your goals or pull you further away from them. Once you identify the habits that are pulling you away from your goals, you must develop a relentless attitude towards changing them. That uncompromising attitude is the difference between merely being involved and actually being committed to the process. In short, being involved is doing what it takes when necessary, while being committed is giving a full effort until whatever goal is achieved.Most times, it is the severity of certain situations that motivate us to do whatever it takes to change. During that time, we become relentless and tap into go-mode. But why wait until the situation gets worse to make a change?

Can you remember a time in your life when you got sick and tired of getting the same results or feeling the same way, and then you made the commitment to change? After that decision was made, nothing was able to stop you until change happened, not death, not ridicule, or being ostracized from the people you love. The only thing that you would accept was change.

I remember my battle with depression in college, and I remember the day I became sick and tired of being sick and tired. At the point of frustration, I became committed to overcoming depression, and what followed great effort was great results. Nothing changed instantaneously, except for my mindset. There were a set of habits that were keeping me stuck in a cycle, and I had to decide in my mind to become committed to the process of changing old habits.

I remember sitting down with a friend from CrossFit, and we were talking before the group class had started. In conversation, she started telling me how she really resonated with a post that I made on social media, where I talked about my battle with depression and how much of a toll it had on me mentally and physically. She began sharing with me how her daily responsibilities had suddenly become daunting tasks. She used to enjoy waking up in the morning and dominating her day, but now, the most challenging part of her day was getting out of bed in the morning after hitting the snooze a couple of times, and then trying to find the energy that she needed to start her day. Just getting up in the morning became a burden.

As she spoke, it brought me back to when I was in a very low place in my life, and when I too struggled to get out of bed. It's interesting though, because I had always considered myself to be an ambitious person, and during those low moments, ambition was nowhere to be found.

There were many mornings where I would wake up and lay in my bed for hours. I would get tired from just thinking about the amount of effort that it took to walk to the bathroom and take a hot shower. As much as I love hot showers in the morning, the work required to get out of bed didn't seem worth it on many occasions. During these low moments, it messed with me that I could not simply find the energy to get out of bed.

At the time, I knew I wasn't well, I knew that I was struggling with depression, but it didn't matter to me. I was only concerned about waking up and doing what I had always done. However, the battle with depression had me feeling paralyzed. It was as if my brain broke, and I could not get my mind and body in sync. I knew exactly what I wanted to do, but I could not do it.

As I continued to listen to my friend speak, I felt empathy and compassion for her because I was once in her shoes, and I felt what she was feeling. As a friend, I listened, shared my experiences, and I offered a few suggestions that worked for me during my battle. But I still understood that she was going to need to become committed to her own process in order to see real results.

We all want to have a sense of achievement. It doesn't matter how big or small. I reassured my friend that it was okay that she could not do everything with the same level of intensity as she did in the past. However, that didn't mean that she should stop doing everything. There were things that she could still commit to, just on a smaller scale.

As you're working to develop new habits and modify old ones, it's important to recognize that it took time to develop the habits that you currently have, and it is going to take time to modify those habits as well.

Modifying your habits is a process that starts with small steps. From taking the small steps and collecting your small wins, you will receive that sense of achievement, which will turn into momentum, and once you have momentum, you will be able to accomplish other tasks. The aim of the game should be doing whatever is necessary to gain momentum because once momentum is gained, it's harder to stop you from moving forward.

Think of a freight train. When it leaves the station, it doesn't start at top speed. It has a slow start, and as the wheels begin to turn, the train begins to pick up speed. Once it reaches its maximum speed, nothing will stop that train. I've seen movies where trains literally run through cars that are on the tracks and still keep going. You must begin to think of yourself as a train. If you can start small and continue to build momentum, you will eventually reach a speed where it will be nearly impossible to stop you. But again, it starts with the small steps.

Although my friend couldn't find the energy to get up early and do a high-intensity workout every day, she could commit to a daily walk. Although she could not stop the negative thoughts from playing in her mind, she could commit to writing 3-5 things that she is grateful for.

It's all about the small wins! Change happens when you can genuinely appreciate your small wins as you're growing through your journey.

Let's do a quick activity. Answer these questions as honestly and clearly as you can:

What is one goal that you would like to achieve within the next five years?

____

____

____

What is one habit that is keeping you from achieving that goal?

____

____

____

What is one habit that you will need to develop to achieve that goal?

____

____

____

As human beings, there are no limitations except the ones that we place in our own minds. According to the Bible, humankind came into existence after God said, "Let us make man in our image, in our likeness (Genesis 1:26)." What does that even mean? Personally, I don't think that this verse is referring to our physical appearance or existence. Instead, I believe that it is confirmation that we are spirit and that God's spirit is inside of us.

Have you ever stopped to consider that God's spirit is in you? God deposited the likeness of his spirit inside of you, and he expects a return on his investment. You can attract what you desire into your life, and it starts with your habits.

After you become clear on where you are and where you want to be, get committed. Decide to do three things that you can do consistently that will take you closer to developing habits that will allow you to manifest your goals into your life.

Example - The Simple 3's:

1. Spread my bed.
2. Complete my morning walk and meditation.
3. Write 3-5 things that I am grateful for.

What are your three things?

The Simple 3's:

1. ______________________________

2. ______________________________

3. ______________________________

Remember, who you are at this moment is a combination of the thoughts you dwell on and your habits. If you are not satisfied with who you are and where you are, then it's time to make a change. Start with your habits.

Chapter 6

Faith Over Fear

"Faith is taking the first step even when you don't see the whole staircase."
-Martin Luther King, Jr.

"For we walk by faith, not by sight"
2 Corinthians 5:7

According to the Oxford dictionary, faith is defined as complete trust or confidence in someone or something. It is also defined as a strong belief in God; or a religious doctrine, based on spiritual apprehensions rather than proof. When you choose to walk by faith, you are making a decision that no matter what happens, and whether you like it or not, you will stay the course until you have reached the desired result or destination. Faith is not just the trust you have in something, but its the action you take based on that trust. Faith is driving home late at night in the dark while it is raining cats and dogs, and you're running low on gas. And although it may seem scary or overwhelming, you choose to believe that you will get home safely. Now, I know this scenario is a bit dramatic, but how might this be considered an exercise of faith? Although there is no proof that you are going to get home safely, you make the active choice to believe that you will, and the action backing your belief was to continue the drive home.

Understand that often choosing faith requires you to combat your fears directly. Using the example of driving home in the rain, yes, it may seem scary to drive home in those conditions, but what happens if you give more power to the thoughts of negative outcomes? You would probably start off by having thoughts of running out of gas and getting stuck in the side of the road, then what would happen if you got stuck on the side of the road. Now you're thinking about how you can't see the lines in the road with the rain and how you might swerve and crash, and at this point, you begin thinking the chances of making it home are slim. That is exactly what you don't need to do, but it happens when you feed fear energy. Both faith and fear require the same amount of energy; it is impossible to be in both states at the same time. I can
prove it.

Close your eyes and think of what you fear the most. This is not to put you into a state of fear, but to combat it as I stated before. Do this for about 10 seconds. Now close your eyes and think about the hopes you have that bring you peace, joy, or happiness, whether it be your plans for the future, your family, or your materials. Do this also for about 10 seconds. Lastly, close your eyes for 10 seconds and try to think about both things simultaneously, what you fear, and what brings you joy and happiness, all within the same thought. You will find that this cannot be done. You cannot be in both states, faith and fear.

We all go through times in our life when we are (for various reasons) in a state of fear. It could be the fear of losing a job, a relationship, or even one's life. Fear is normal; although it is unpleasant, everyone experiences it. Fear is an emotion caused by the belief that someone or something is dangerous, likely to cause pain, or a threat. Fear is an emotion that you will feel throughout life; however, how you react to it will play a role in your life's possibilities and outcomes. Many people are fearful because of the unknown, the feeling and thought that something is greater than their control and that it will harm or cause them pain. The acronym I give to the word fear is False Evidence Appearing Real. This is a reminder that although it may feel real, that does not mean that it is. On the other hand, when you have faith, you believe in the greater good. You believe in your heart and mind that the end result you desire will happen, although you may not see it, feel it, or like it, you genuinely believe that every step along the journey will bring you to your destination.

When you live with the mindset and attitude that your faith is greater than any fear, you start to realize the power behind the words and belief. Once you understand this, the actions behind just saying "I have faith" will start to show. You will have fewer worries and more understanding, and you will not let fear hold you back from experiencing certain things in life. When it comes to this, people will sometimes say, "fake it until you make it." This does not mean to be dishonest, but you should act like whatever is going on around you is not just a coincidence, that it was meant to happen. You may not have all the clarity you need to feel comfortable, and it may not make sense in the moment, but when you look back, you'll have that "ah-ha" moment and then be able to say, "I see you God, I see what you did there."

God has blessed me with experiences throughout my life that have done nothing but build my faith from the ground up. I did not always know why at the time, but the "ah-ha" moment always finds a way to pop back into my life. At the age of 18, I moved over two hundred miles away from home to Orlando, with no close friends or family. Did I know what I was doing? No. Did I know all the obstacles that I would run into? No. Was I scared? Most certainly. But without a doubt, I did know that no matter what, I had an amazing God that was walking with me and guiding me every step of the way.

Before finalizing the move, I made sure to confirm that I would be able to relocate my job, and thankfully, I was. After a few months of working at the new store, I got promoted to "Lead" (technically a supervisor, just without the title) at another location that was 16 miles away from my home. I took on the new role and responsibilities with no problems until problems started to find me. After a couple of months of driving back and forth to work, over 30 miles a day, my car started to have serious issues. Sometimes it would not start, some days the a/c would not work, but what topped it all off was when my windows; driver and passenger, were constantly falling –yes, falling. There were days when I would be driving to or from work in the rain, and then the windows would drop. So now I'm driving on the highway trying to hold up my window with one hand, all while getting wet, sometimes even soaked. My car gave out completely after a while, and I was relying on Lyfts and Ubers every day, spending anywhere from $40-$45 roundtrip for work. Be mindful that I was only making about $90/day before tax too. I used to go home and cry so often, and sometimes I even questioned God why me. This was probably the most that I ever made working, but for almost half to go to transportation alone, I was in the hole. I was always behind on rent, getting around was a challenge, and I did not have money to do anything besides survive. To top it all off, I was now faced with demoting myself back to a sales rep so I could be closer to home just to save money. But wait, it does not stop there.

At the time, I could feel the shift happening in my life but nothing was going according to plan. Fear crept in and consumed me. "What else could go wrong?" "I did all this work and ended up demoting myself, why me?" were questions I repeatedly asked myself and God. I then remembered my plan is not always the plan God has for me and I was able to build my faith knowing so. After going back to that store, (a company I was devoted to for over three years,) I requested a very important day off, November 22nd, which is the date my father passed. Usually, if someone agrees to cover your shift, then you are approved off. In this case, because I was still skilled for a lead, they did not want me to switch with anyone else unless they were also an official lead. That same day, I quit.

Now here I was quitting a job with no backup plan or anything lined up, and a lot of people would say that's crazy, but God showed me my worth. No money is enough for me to stay somewhere I feel disrespected and undervalued. Although I did not know what I was going to do, I knew God had more for me. Something better.

"When you have a plan or a vision, write it down and then pray on it."

I was struggling financially, but I had a friend that I ended up being roommates with, and for a while, we helped support each other. Not to say it was easy, but it was definitely a blessing. At that time, I was still going to school full time and now working two part-time jobs, but having a roommate made it a bit easier. Although I struggled a bit and had to be placed in a few uncomfortable situations, I felt like through it all God was using me and not only for me, but also for me to share my story with others. After doing what I believed was my purpose in Orlando – getting my associates degree in college, and meeting certain people– God had plans for me to go back home.

Fast forward to two years later. I am now working at a job similar to what I was doing prior, sales. The difference is its telecommunication sales. Now don't let me fool you; being a sales consultant isn't the easiest. It can sometimes get a bit overwhelming, especially when trying to convince people to see the value of purchasing a product from you. So that, plus working in a call center with a lot of different energies and vibes going around, it was just a bit too much for my anxiety. I started to lose focus at work, and it showed. My sales were not as high as they were before, and I struggled to hit all the other metrics that we aim to achieve. I loved my job, but it was obvious that I needed a break. During this period, I took a leap of faith and decided to take time off work to recollect and get myself together. I used this time to invest in myself, and I decided to sign up for something I was interested in, bartending school. In the course, I learned about different wines and liquors, practice making specialty drinks, work on time efficiency, and proper bartending etiquette. That experience was an entire journey, and I would not change anything about it. That honestly was the final push that I needed to start my business, Jell-E Shots!

After receiving my bartending license, I took what started off as something that I just enjoyed doing as a hobby and turned it into a business. Jell-E Shots started from me making jello shots for myself and a few friends and family. It then progressed to making jello shots for a friend who was hosting networking events and small parties. After catering to a few of these events, my name started to get out there, and I decided to really take it seriously. With the help of my younger brother, we came up with the name Jell-E Shots. Unique yet catchy. The "E" does not only symbolize my name, but it also symbolizes what I do/make – everything. It started with Jell-E cups, to now syringes, drinks, bottles, slushies, and more.

When I first started, my mom used to question me on why I chose to do this sort of business. "Why alcohol?" "You think people will pay that price?" "I think you're just doing it for fun."

Things like that would discourage me at times, but I was confident in the vision that God had for me, and if it wasn't for my faith and confidence, I would not have made it this far. At the time, my mom did not see and understand the passion and the joy that I got from making drinks. As a Haitian parent, she was more so worried about if I was making money or not, and being honest, for a long time I was not. But guess what? I did not mind because I truly enjoy making drinks and the opportunity it gives me to interact with so many amazing people. This business has allowed me to meet and mingle with over two hundred different people from networking and vendor events, as well as the amazing customer referrals that I get. It has only been a year and a half since I officially launched my business, but I am so grateful that I started, and I have come so far. This is still only the beginning, but I cannot stop imagining the other great things that God has in store for me.

When you have a plan or a vision, write it down and then pray on it. Ask God to direct you and give you clarity on the things you have spoken of and asked for. Writing things down can help in so many ways. Not only is it soothing, but it allows you to have, sort of like a blueprint or outline of what is really going on in your mind and heart. I devote my first twenty to thirty minutes of my day to writing to God. Now when I write, I make sure it relates to nothing but positivity, goals, aspirations, prayers, and things that I envision in my life. Have you ever heard of the saying, "the tongue holds power?" To me, it's kind of the same when it comes to writing, especially if you are like me, and you go back to read your writing aloud. Whatever you speak over your life has a huge possibility of happening. I remember the beginning of 2018, I made my first vision board. (If you are unfamiliar, a vision board is usually a collage of images, quotes, and affirmations used to create/represent your goals and dreams.) My vision board consisted of many things that year from eating healthier, working out, working on saving, traveling, and a few other things. On my vision board I wrote that I wanted to travel to a different place every month. With writing it down, talking to God, and praying about it, everything started to play out right before my eyes.

In one year, I traveled to Orlando, Philadelphia, Atlanta Cayman Islands, New York, and Key West. I also went to Nicaragua with a group of young ladies who I did not know prior to the trip, and I was very fearful. I was scared because I joined a travel group off of social media, and at the time, I did not know anyone that was going at all. I was also scared because we would be traveling to another country where English was not the primary language, and I was concerned about being able to communicate. Would I be able to translate certain things? What if I got sick? Who will I go to for help? All these thoughts were making me build fear, but I started to pray and ask God for guidance and clarity. I walked by faith and put my concerns to the side, and that four-day trip ended up being one of the best trips of my life, hands down. Those trips and experiences really opened my eyes to see that whatever you want in life is possible, especially when you write it down, continue to speak life into it, and get God involved through prayer. Do not allow fear to control you. Having faith will truly allow you to manifest anything you want in life.

Chapter 7

Your Perspective Controls Your Reality

"To change ourselves effectively, we first had to change our perceptions."
-Stephen R. Covey

"The only thing you sometimes have control over is your perspective. You don't have control over your situation. But you have a choice about how you view it."
-Chris Pine

How do you see life?

Question:
Why do you eat cereal with milk?

You are probably thinking, "who starts a chapter like this...?" But, I really need to know your answer. Email me your answer to info@timonebrown.com right now!

Did you answer this question by saying something like, "Because it's good..."

"I don't know..."

"I like it like that."

"Because it's what I was told"

"It's what you're supposed to do."

It's interesting how people do many things but really don't know why they do it. Many times you could say that it's almost automatic. For instance, if over the years starting with your childhood you were told that "riding a bicycle is dangerous," and during that time, saw instances where this was valid, like say – seeing someone fall off their bicycle and cry. Without even knowing why they fell, you'd attribute it to what you've always heard, "bicycles are dangerous" you now believe bicycles are dangerous. And now, as an adult you teach your children the same thing, when in reality riding a bicycle is one of the safest modes of transportation.

So how can one change their perspectives of life? Well, you have to start asking yourself questions and giving yourself transparent answers. I know somebody that's reading this thinks that the cereal and milk question does not make sense. It's cool. You're entitled to think what you want to think, but I'm telling you now, why you felt that way is shaped by your perspective.

As you read this chapter, the only favor I ask of you is to be willing to ask yourself the hard questions and be ready to reconsider some things.

Before we get started, let's define "perspective." Grab your phone, ask Siri or Google search for the definition. It's important that you do this yourself before reading the definition I have below.

The definition of perspective:

- In the late 14th century it was defined as "science of optics."

- Google search definition number 2., "a particular attitude toward or way of regarding something; a point of view."

- My definition: "How you decide to see life."

(Did you actually research the definition yourself or did you keep reading? Yes _____ or No _____)

In order for us to understand the way we view life, we have to be willing to question everything –including our upbringing, our parents and the society we live in. Our perspectives are shaped by what we have been exposed to throughout our life, starting with our experiences as children. Our parents, the people around us, and the environments we were exposed to would significantly impact how we see and experience everything. Because of this, everything that you think you know or what you learned growing up could very well not serve your well-being, although you once thought it did. In order to progress and shift your mindset, it is essential to question what we once or currently believe.

Your "right" can be another person's "wrong?"

Your "up" can be another person's "down?"

Your "success" can be another person's "failure?"

Your "love" can be another person's "hate?"

So what's your perspective? Who and what has shaped your viewpoint? Think. Where are you from? Did you grow up with money or not? Did you experience more positive environments than negative? What were you taught to believe? What do you believe now? How is this controlling the narrative of your life?

So many questions can be asked to the point that it can become overwhelming. I know exactly how that feels, and if you are in that headspace, take a deep breath. Although at the moment, you may feel like you cannot control or change the way you perceive certain situations, I am a walking testimony that you can. You have the power to change the way you see the world around you.

I remember when I began to question life heavily after my mother's death during my senior year in high school. It seemed that her death opened up a gateway to numerous challenges that continued long after my graduation; from losing love, to dropping out of college for a year, to becoming the legal guardian of my younger sister at the age of 19. It just seemed that my circumstances were piling on top of each other, and that my life was going in a downward spiral. Can you relate? Not to my particular situation, but to the constant application of pressure by life?

Have you ever gotten to the point where you asked, "Why is this happening to me?"

Yes _____ or No _____

Life happens, but it doesn't happen to you. There are experiences that you can control and there are many you can't, but no matter what your experience in life is, you possess the power of choice. Most people struggle to accept this and dwell upon what they can't control, instead of empowering themselves where they have the ability to make a decision. Life continuously happens and circumstances will always appear, no matter how successful or miserable you are. I teach people to shift their perspective, because it's one of the only aspects of life we can control. I could only imagine the life I'd currently have if I used my mother's death as a reason to become stuck in negative thoughts and behaviors. Instead I chose not to be life's victim, although it was not easy, I had to become aware and continuously work on shifting my perspective. My perspective of life could have been completely skewed by the insecurities created during some of my most harrowing experiences.

To some, those experiences validate a pessimistic and negative thought process; it also validates a victim mindset. This thought process completely negates a person's ability to be an agent of change. That type of thinking gives away your power to choose what happens to your life instead of reinforcing it. Yet, to others, it becomes motivation or fuel to live life with purpose. It's all a matter of choice. It's all a matter of perspective.
Success and failure are a part of life. Ups and downs are both going to happen. Wins and losses will occur. However, the only thing that matters as you experience these circumstances is your power to make a decision. You decide how you see life, and you decide how you will allow these experiences to affect you, YOU DECIDE.

Cry, hurt, feel the pain, but at the same time choose to dominate life, or it will dominate you.

I'll give you an example of one of my student's, MJ, and you take a moment to ponder what his perspective of life may be.

MJ's Life

MJ's mother and father had a nasty break up when he was young and his father stopped being involved after the break up. Since the relationship ended, his mother holds anger and resentment towards his father. When she looks at MJ she sees his dad. Every day MJ's mother takes her resentment for his father out on him. And though he loves her, he can't stand that he makes her feel that way. She consistently verbally assaults him and though he would never disrespect her, this has poorly affected MJ's perspective of women. MJ begins to respond negatively towards women in power because he cannot fully understand why his mom is treating him this way.

School is MJ's escape, he's one of the "cool" kids and a football player. He's not popular because he is trying to be, MJ has natural leadership qualities that people are attracted to. Sometimes he feels like there's a certain reputation he must live up to, and his personal issues will mess that up if his peers find out. Until one day, MJ snapped and let his emotions out on a teacher that raised her voice as she criticized him in front of the class. See, because of his maladaptive perspective due to what was going on at home, he couldn't respond appropriately to his reality. How he viewed this teacher or any woman that would raise their voice was a threat.

Even though this was just an example, this illustrates how our perspective can affect how we act and react to the things that happen in our lives. Our perspectives and the variables within each are different, of course, but if we don't take the time to debrief what we've experienced, we'll carry old (or outdated) thoughts, feelings and learned behaviors into the new things that are constantly taking place. I mean actually think about it! What happened to MJ at home influenced his perspective and thus his actions toward his teacher. What we have to realize is that MJ's perspective has been shaped by everything going on outside of him and not by himself. If someone is not aware of how and why their perspective (what they think and how they feel) is the way it is, it can drastically impact their life. MJ isn't the only person who holds to perspectives that don't serve him, but just like MJ, how we decide to see life is strictly up to us.

MJ's decisions are his own, but if he is not self aware he can be influenced by people, environments, or even situations. If MJ depends strictly on outside validation, whether it's another person's opinion of him or what he sees going on around him, before making a decision, he's not honoring himself. And the same is true for us.

When it comes to understanding your perspective and shifting it, self awareness is essential. If MJ became aware that the only reason his mom is treating him badly is because of her being hurt by his father, he could reason more and be understanding. This would help remove his generalized thoughts about women, allowing him to receive criticism from them without taking it too personal. It would also free up a portion of himself that he's hid in an attempt to not be vulnerable.

I told you about MJ to get you thinking about how your own perspectives can control your actions and your reality. I want you to understand that just by being aware, you have the power to shift not only your perspective but your life!

1) What is your perspective of the world? I really want you to think about this fully and write in full detail below!

____

____

____

____

____

____

____

2) What has caused you to have this view? Think about the experiences, people, and places, maybe even if the news had anything to do with it? List it all below.

"Instead I chose not to be life's victim"

After writing down your answers to the previous two questions, does your perspective of the world serve you? When I say this, I really want you to look deep. Does it make you happy or sad? Is your view full of abundance and wealth or poverty and lack? You are not at fault for the perspective you had before reading this, but if that perspective no longer serves you on your journey to becoming it is your right and obligation to shift it!

Chapter 8

Let It Go
So You Can Grow

What are you holding onto that is no longer serving you?

This is a crucial question to ask yourself if you are committed to growth. It is equally important that you be brutally honest when you ask yourself this question also. There are things from your past that will come up when you ponder this, things that you can no longer ignore. Asking yourself this question will also bring you face-to-face with the challenge and opportunity to address your enemy (a.k.a. your inner me). Trust me when I say life changes for you when you accept that challenge and embrace that opportunity.

As you read this chapter, read with an open heart and mind, and make sure you have your pen ready. If you experience intense emotions while working through this, please pause and revisit it at a different time. And if necessary, please work with a mental health professional to help you through the process of revisiting your past. This work is to put yourself in a position to take back control over your life. You can't go forward and truly prosper unless you let go of and grow from your past. My entire life changed the day I decided to accept this challenge.

I was probably 11 or 12 years old when I started to keenly watch my parents and identify the things that I knew I did not want to repeat when I got older. In my heart, I felt that there were things that I heard and saw that were not right, but because of my naiveté and immaturity, I suppressed the way I felt while growing up. I developed the habit, and quite frankly, the skill of masking my true emotions. It took years, but I eventually became masterful at it. So much so, I couldn't even identify with how I really felt anymore. It was all a blur of many different emotions on one canvas.

So, my parents met in their 20's while living in Jamaica and decided it was best to move to the United States in 1994 to build their family. About a year after moving, I was born. Just like all parents, mom and dad had their challenges, especially being immigrants in a new country, but unbeknownst to all of us kids (4 of us at the time). There were no indications that those challenges were big enough to cause them to separate. But after over 20 years of being married, my parents' marriage ended in divorce. They were officially separated when I was 15, and that rocked my world. From all that was going on in our family at the time, I developed a deep level of apathy towards the world and everyone around me. My favorite line was, "I don't care." But if you dug deep beyond what I was portraying on the surface, even a child could see that I did care... I cared a lot. I just chose to hide it. Before their separation, I had this perfect image of our family and what we would look like in the future. What we'd do together, the places we'd visit, and all the fun and memories we'd make; all of it was shattered in my teenage years. During their fights, I would be fed information from both of my parents about one another, and I felt trapped in the middle of a never-ending cycle of negative thoughts and feelings towards them. At the time, there was no way that I could have known what the effects of the divorce would have had on me, but now in my early 20's, I'm still working through the aftermath of what happened years ago.

After the divorce, I became an angry kid. I stopped caring about a lot of things, and I let myself come out of character. I felt betrayed by my parents, more specifically, by my dad. I believed that he didn't care about the hurt that I was feeling from the divorce. I also believed that he was the one who was wrong and that he was the cause for all that was happening to break up our family during that time. Because I held strongly to this belief, I hated my dad. Not only did I hate him, but I wanted him to feel it whenever I was around him. These feelings grew as I grew older and later put us in an estranged relationship where we barely spoke.

After graduating from high school, I moved away for college in 2014 and thought that I could run away from dealing with the hurt and betrayal that I felt inside. And for a while, if you were on the outside looking in, I did a great job. You could never catch me without a smile on my face, I always found a way to help and counsel others, and I had a strong work ethic that I used to disguise what I felt internally. Working harder and adding more to my plate was my drug of choice.

I didn't want to ever think about the divorce and its effect on me ever again, but the older I got, the more it showed up. I'd watch a sentimental movie and be triggered by a father-son scene. I'd have a conversation with my girlfriend at the time and suddenly be filled with emotions. The more I matured, I realized that I couldn't run from the pain any longer. I had to address it head-on.

The pain and betrayal that I felt as a teenage boy was keeping me from being the best version of myself in every area of my life, especially in my intimate relationship with my now wife. Something had to change, and I had to accept the challenge and opportunity to grow through a season of my life that has played a huge role in shaping who I was up until that point. A different result required me to do something different, and the same is true for you. For you to continue your journey of growth and development, you will have to become someone totally different.

Through therapy, prayer, and a willingness to step into the unknown and uncomfortable territory, I have been able to work through my feelings of anger and betrayal towards my dad. I rebuilt a relationship that was necessary to move forward.

If you're ready to walk through the steps of letting go of your past to grow from it, take some time to work through these questions and statements with the same brutal honesty that I spoke of earlier:

1. Reflect on and explain one event that happened in your past that has caused you to feel betrayed, damaged, rejected, or abused.

   ____
   ____
   ____
   ____

2. How has that event shaped the person you are today and how does it affect the way you treat yourself and others?

   ____
   ____
   ____
   ____

3. Do you have any triggers that bring you back to the state of mind you were in at the time of the event? List them. (i.e. "Stay" by Rihanna reminds me of a bad break-up)

____

____

____

____

4. List all of the reasons why your feelings are valid?

____

____

____

____

5. Explain why moving forward is important?

____

____

____

____

6. Create a positive affirmation that will help you to combat the negative thoughts when they show up.

____

____

____

____

7. Who can you surround yourself with or trust to hold you accountable if you start to slip into the past? List as many names as you can.

____

____

An exercise that may be helpful for you is to write a letter. Here's how it works: set a date and time (a few hours, maybe even a full day) where you will write to the person or thing that brought you the pain. While writing, give yourself permission to express everything that you feel. Write about the anger, disgust, and resentment that you have been holding onto for so long. After getting everything out on paper (through the tears and cuss words), you can burn the letter, tear it up, or do whatever you want with it. The letter is purposely for you. Your feelings and emotions are worth expressing, and sometimes the greatest way to express them is through writing.

I am a huge advocate for therapy and people doing what is necessary for their mental health. If you find that you need help with expressing or articulating your emotions, please invest in a therapist. Therapy has changed the game for me on so many levels!

As you put the work in to let go and grow from your past, be patient with yourself, and understand that you will become stronger and better because of your efforts. I celebrate you for accepting the challenge and opportunity to continue your journey. You're one step closer!

Chapter 9

There's Power in Self-Realization

"Men can starve from a lack of self-realization as much as they can from a lack of bread."
-Richard Wright

"Your own self-realization is the greatest service you can render the world."
-Ramana Maharshi

The Road 2 Spiritual Success, if comprehended, allowed you to be introspective and take a reflective look inward. To be able to shift your life and become a better version of yourself, introspection is more than necessary.

If you look at the world's current state, there is still so much healing needing to be done. There's a saying that goes, "doing the same thing over again expecting different results is insanity." Insanity being a disordered state of mind. Collectively, our world has been in this disordered state of mind for generations, regardless of race.

If we take a look in ourselves individually, putting things into perspective, we can, if willing and open, see the underlying root of the problems we face today. Earlier in the book, I spoke of love. Love is something we must understand and possess; it is the foundation.

Look at the foundation of your current state, is it built on love?

I can turn on the news, and not even 15 minutes into it, I can tell you that there is a void of love. The world we live in was built on war, violence, and slavery, among many other ills. That is not love.

How could there be health crises if we love one another, cherishing ourselves according to its true definition? How can there be racism or murders if we love one another? There cannot be! Just as music removes silence and light removes darkness, love removes hate. They cannot co-exist; it is not possible.

Understanding, comprehending, and putting this, in addition to all the topics learned in this book to practice, will shift the way you forever see yourself and your potential. You will begin to see yourself for the King or Queen you truly are. This is the power of self-realization- the act of achieving the full development of your potential.

With the exception of a few, most are ignorant of their potential due to various reasons such as generational conditioning and their environments. All of which leads to a life full of mediocrity, never allowing one to really experience the abundance of what life has to offer.

To help you understand, I will use "The Elephant Rope" story by Robert Terson as an example.

"As a man was passing the elephants, he suddenly stopped, confused by the fact that these huge creatures were being held by only a small rope tied to their front leg. No chains, no cages. It was obvious that the elephants could, at anytime, break away from their bonds but for some reason, they did not. He saw a trainer nearby and asked why these animals just stood there and made no attempt to get away. "Well," trainer said, "when they are very young and much smaller we use the same size rope to tie them and, at that age, it's enough to hold them. As they grow up, they are conditioned to believe they cannot break away. They believe the rope can still hold them, so they never try to break free." The man was amazed. These animals could at any time break free from their bonds but because they believed they couldn't, they were stuck right where they were."

Elephants are one of the strongest animals in the world, but because they were conditioned since birth not to know their true strength and their true potential, a small rope will always hold their potential captive.

Another great example is the "Fable of the Eagle and the Chicken." An eagle fell out of its nest and was found and raised by a farmer around chickens. As it grew older it followed its environment; the eagle would peck the ground like a chicken and walk like a chicken too. Although an eagle, it mentally became a chicken because of its upbringing and environment. It was not until the eagle was removed from its environment that it realized its true potential and began to soar on the heights.

Just like the elephant and the eagle, many of us are held back by a small rope or our surroundings. When this is understood and you realize who you are, there is no rope that can hold you, and no environment can cap your potential. All shackles will break, and you will then begin to soar how you were born to.

As the great book says, "No weapon formed against you shall prosper." You have limitless potential. Coach Roc addressed you as you should be–Kings and Queens– remember you were born to prosper. You are made in the image of the creator. You can do ALL things!

Chapter 10

In the Image of The Creator

"So God created mankind in his own image, in the image of God he created them; male and female he created them."
-Genesis 1:27

Would I be correct if I said that many of us have been programmed to feel as if life is happening to us instead of for us? There is this myth that I also once believed; that our creator is some puppet master pulling all the strings in our lives, and we have no control over how our life goes.

As I've grown, I have come to realize that I am in control of the reality around me, and more times than not, I have created it in some way, shape, or form. The quote from Genesis 1:27 (which is also under the chapter title) really went over my head until about two years ago. It states:

"So God created mankind in his own image, in the image of God he created them; male and female he created them."

If our creator created us in his own image, this means we too have the ability to create. Many times throughout life we can feel as if we cannot change what is going on around us, not realizing we were actually born to do that very thing. We become victims to the lives we were meant to be victors in.

That which you feel yourself to be, you are. The question to ask yourself is, "Who am I?" If the answer is anything but extraordinary, abundant, and beautiful, create it. Create yourself an extraordinary, abundant life with a beautiful self-image. You might be thinking, "How does one recreate their life?" To aid in answering this question, I will provide a short story of Heath Ledger.

Heath Ledger was a young global phenom in the world of performing arts. The world was forever changed after his iconic role as "The Joker" in the 150+ award-winning film The Dark Knight. In becoming The Joker, Heath locked himself in a room for one month to recreate himself as The Joker. He read all of the Batman comics and trained himself to think like The Joker to the point that while on set, he encouraged Christian Bale to physically harm him so it could be more authentic. Heath was so obsessed with his role in the film that one could even say he became The Joker.

In the world of performing arts, thespians (actors) are always recreating themselves to play a role. We must take a page from their book when it comes to our lives. Think of your life as a library of films; every chapter in your life a new movie –movies in which we are not just the leading actor, but also the director. We can not limit ourselves to the last movie or creative work that was made because we can always get better and we can always create more! If we continue to harp on what we have created in the past, we will never be able to create our futures without reliving them. When creating on your journey, be very mindful of the following. Although these are not the end-all be-all, just being aware of these four points will aid tremendously!

1. Utilize your senses!

When you read this step, what was the first thing to come to mind? Was it taste, feel, hear, see, or smell? If so, you are correct, partially. If you are blessed with all five senses, understand that these senses are not just to taste food, see your favorite movie, or hear your favorite tune. As a creator, you can utilize the tools creating those senses: the mouth, ears, eyes, body, and nose, to aid you on your journey of becoming! I am going to reference three of the five tools you use for your senses; the mouth, ears, and eyes, and how they can affect and benefit you.

Mouth

Let's start with your mouth! Of course, our mouth can be used to tell us if our meal is yummy or disgusting, but have you ever thought about using it to speak life onto what you desire? Growing up, I can always think back to saying something that was not so pleasant and an adult stating to me, "Watch your mouth!" At the time, I did not know that those words would play a role in my life today. When you hear the phrase "Watch your mouth!" the first thing that comes to mind is probably someone using profanity. And although you are correct, allow me to challenge your perspective a little further. Think of every word that comes from your mouth as if it had the power of a spell, and that every time you speak, you're casting a new spell that in some way, shape, or form will indefinitely manifest.

In the first chapter, we expressed how important it is to speak love and positivity over yourself. You have to do the same thing for the life you desire to have, for the you you are becoming. In the bible, Proverbs 18:21 states, "The tongue has the power of life and death..." Understand that everything you fix your mouth to say has the power to create. Whether it is positive or negative, you will reap the words you have sewn into the universe. If you are familiar with the Christian religion, you know God's infamous words, "Let there be light" then the light was created. God used words to create light and bring life into the world. Now if you were to look at your words as spells, then anything that is not positive or useful for creating joy would be considered a curse, negating the blessing you truly desire in any given situation. Stop putting curses on your life with your words.

Have you ever had an outcome that did not go your way, and you think to yourself, "I said this would happen."? Well, ding, ding, ding! Of course it didn't. You created it with negative talk. You have to become disciplined when it comes to the words you say. When you decide to use your tongue to speak, you will eventually reap the consequences of whatever was said; good or bad. Do not speak negatively over your life; speak good things over your life, and over everything in it.

When speaking to create your life, you have to speak as if it is happening. You also have to know what you desire; there is power in clarity!

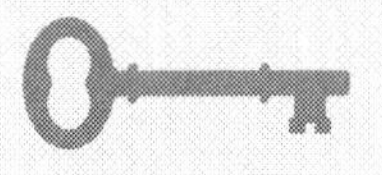

I want you to stop exactly where you are and write out 26 declaring positive affirmations about yourself using adjectives from every letter in the alphabet from A-Z. When writing out your affirmations, do so in the format of "I am" statements, for example, "I am amazing," "I am beautiful." "I am" is a declaration that what was of the past will no longer serve your future.
Read your affirmations first thing in the morning everyday. And when you feel as if they are not working, continue reading them; that's where your faith will play a big role. And when you feel as if you have accomplished them, continue to read them, so they remain who you are. You do this every day because you are gifted with the present, so you want to open it up with the right words.

Ears

What your ears hear the most will start to manifest itself into your emotional well being and in your life. Allow me to make sense of this; if someone grows up and has been hearing the phrase "life is not fair" all the time since birth, then they will always create a life that isn't fair, not by choice, but due to the power that lies in what you hear. This person will always find ways to validate that statement, most times, subconsciously. They will begin to listen to music that agrees to what they've always heard and identify with the negative viewpoints that align; this not only validates, but also creates a life that isn't fair. And vice versa. If that same person grew up hearing words like, "All things are working for your good, life is amazing!" They, too, will always find ways to validate it. They would start to move as if life is amazing, and start to position themselves in ways that agree, thus creating themselves a happy life!

Although this is not the only channel we hear messages through, I strategically used music to illustrate the way we use our ears and the power that hearing has to influence. Just being mindful of the music you listen to can aid tremendously in what you create.

I want you to write down your ten most played songs, not your favorites, but most played. Then I want you to analyze what these songs represent.

Do they represent love, happiness, and abundance? Or do they represent heartbreak, depression, and anger? Make sure to be completely honest with yourself and complete this exercise before moving on!

- ______________________________

- ______________________________
- ______________________________
- ______________________________
- ______________________________
- ______________________________
- ______________________________
- ______________________________
- ______________________________
- ______________________________

What do all these songs represent?

____

If all your songs represent the life you wish to create for yourself, awesome! Continue to listen and create what you've always wanted. If not, it is okay. You simply did not know. But now that you do know, I have a 30-day challenge for you! For 30 days, delete the first 7 out of 10 of those songs from your playlist and replace them with songs that will uplift, empower, and aid in the life you want to create!

Which seven songs will you listen to the most for the next 30 days?

- ______________________________
- ______________________________
- ______________________________
- ______________________________
- ______________________________
- ______________________________
- ______________________________

Eyes

What you see tends to play a detrimental role in what you create in your life. Isn't it ironic that in the word eyes is the word yes? I happen to think it validates the thought that what you see, you believe. Read that line again! Haven't we seen this happen on a regular basis? Someone starts watching the news often and begins to feel as if what they are watching is their reality. Growing up, I remember my mom's car being broken into multiple times. See, my mom was always watching the news, and it would continuously portray the world as evil by showing violence, and abductions, and car break-ins repeatedly. As I grew conscious of the power of the things I see with my eyes, it started to make sense as to why the car was constantly being broken into. My mom always watched the news, so what she saw eventually began to present itself in her life.

Social media is used across the globe by any and everyone ranging from infants to senior citizens. Presently, the coronavirus and police brutality are flooding the timelines of all major social media platforms. It is in our best interest as creators to be mindful of how much negativity you allow your eyes to be exposed to.

I want you to scroll down your timeline. If what you see isn't adding value to your life or it's creating unwanted emotions, unfollow, unsubscribe, and delete them from your feed. Then begin to feed your eyes what will satisfy the life you want to create. Follow and subscribe to positive pages, pages that will promote happiness and abundance. Follow pages that you know will help you on your journey.

You may have heard of a vision board, a collage of images and words representing a person's wishes or goals, intended to serve as inspiration or motivation. For this part of the exercise you are to create a visual environment! Print pictures of the life you imagine for yourself, cars, clothes, business, and finances and put it all around you. You want to condition your eyes to see what you will have because you are intentionally creating it.

---

2. Begin with the End in Mind

Often, when thinking about what we truly desire in life, we can become sidetracked by all that is going on during our day-to-day routines. Your worries or concerns might consist of bills, the pandemic, or even a loved one, but it is our duty as the director of our lives to stay focused and remember where we want to go in our lives no matter what happens.

In order to remember where you want to go, you have to know where you want to go. I do a practice every morning where I write down what I truly want with gratitude as if it has already happened. I also do this whenever I start getting discouraged by my circumstances. For example, suppose my goal is to make one million dollars a year. In that case, I'd write down "I am so happy and grateful now that I am making one million dollars per year." Then I would close my eyes and visualize how my life would be affected by my desire, the emotions I feel, the smiles on the face of the people around me, and all the things I am able to bless others with because I am blessed with this desire. If you always move with the end in mind, you will no longer concern yourself with the unfruitfulness of the past. You will begin to live today, planting your seeds for tomorrow.

3. Believe

As a creator, you have the ability to do whatever it is you want to do, but first, you must believe that you can do it. Muhammad Ali said, "To be a great champion, you must believe you are the best." Oprah Winfrey says, "You don't become what you want, you become what you believe." I highlight these respected individuals because they both, Oprah and Muhammad, share the same "rags to riches" storyline. Although they walked two very different paths, they both are great representations of the power of belief.

Answer the following questions. What do you believe about yourself? Do you believe you can achieve and receive all that your heart desires? Do you believe you are deserving of the life you want to create? If you answered yes, or positively to any of the previous questions, I agree with you. If you answered no or negatively, I agree with you also.

You might be thinking how can I agree with both sides? Well, whatever you believe, you give power to. So, if you do not believe you are deserving of the life you want to create, you will never create it because you do not believe you should. Whether good or bad, it is the power of belief and the faith behind that belief that allows things to happen in our life. Remember, you are in control of what you believe about yourself, and there is no better time than right now to change what you believe about, and for yourself.

4. Protect Your InnerG

The law of conservation given by Albert Einstein states, "Energy cannot be created or destroyed, it can only be changed from one form to another." To put this into context, you do not get rid of frustration or sadness, you simply change it to joy or happiness. You are the creator. What are you creating by the words you speak? What do you believe about yourself? Where the mind goes, energy flows. The awareness of how you are feeling and the actions taken to adjust those emotions will be the catalyst to creating the outcome to the life you desire. Protect your innerG!

You may be thinking, "You spelled that wrong." Nope! I spelled it exactly how you read it. The reason being, the word energy derives from two Greek words, en- meaning "in or within" and -ergon meaning "work", think of a car engine although you know it is working you cannot see how it is because all the work is done inside the engine. Just like a car engine the work begins within. What is within manifests without, so I emphasize the "inner" in energy as a constant reminder that it all starts within. When you see the G in "innerG" understand you are the "G." The G stands for anything that you put in the work for; it can mean God, or gratitude, whatever that is for you, it needs to be protected.

There may have been times in your life where you felt as if you had no control over what was going on, to the point you may have even felt like giving up. It is time you take back that control! You are the creator's highest form of creation, created in its image. Use that to your advantage and create yourself the life you truly desire.

Chapter 11

Freedom of Choice, You've Got This!

"Freedom of choice is more to be treasured than any possession Earth can give."
-David O. Mckay

"Emancipate yourselves from mental slavery. None but ourselves can free our minds."
-Bob Marley

"Control your own destiny or someone else will"
-Jack Welch

"It isn't until you come to a spiritual understanding of who you are - not necessarily a religious feeling, but deep down, the spirit within - that you can begin to take control."
-Oprah Winfrey

If you are reading this, we are proud of you, and you should be proud of yourself! Many people buy books, less start them, and even less finish them, but here you are in the last chapter. There is a saying that goes, "knowledge is power", and while knowledge is very resourceful, it does not become power until applied. The *Road to Spiritual Success* is not a book you read and you forget about. It is a journey of practice, practicing to better yourself. From so many great reads such as *"Think and Grow Rich: A Black Choice"* by Dennis Kimbro and Napoleon Hill, and *"Spiritual Principles for a Prosperous Life"* by Robert Henderson Jr., I have learned that your income rarely exceeds your personal development. To put it plainly, the better you become, the better your pockets become, to say the least.

As I have stated earlier in the book, throughout your journey do not forget the foundation– love. This will be important every second of the way. This is definitely the road less traveled, but thankfully, this is not a hard road to embark on. It's not easy either. I like to think it is rather simple, you just have to do it.

Along this road you may find bumps. You may even want to turn around and go back the way you came. It will test your will, character, and faith during these challenging moments, and you will have to give yourself constant reassuring love, without judgment. But I assure you, those who stay the course on the road less traveled that come across the riches less found.
When I use the word "riches", it is more than just money. It is peace and happiness within. It is the newfound love that you have for yourself and life in general. It is what turns your complaints into gratitude, transforming you from hopeless to hopeful. And if monetary riches are what you seek, then you have a new way of looking for them. Through the lenses of wealth, love, and abundance rather than poverty and lack. Now that you have made it thus far, you have a choice to make. No longer a choice from a state of ignorance, but a choice from a place of awareness.

Throughout this book (if utilized correctly), you were able to take notes for you to continue to study. From love to self-realization, these are notes that will– with practice, unlock the doors to more opportunities than ever imagined. We hope that the *Road to Spiritual Success* has evolved your way of thinking about yourself and your life.

In the great book, Romans chapter 12, verse 2 says, "Do not conform to the pattern of this world, but be transformed by the renewing of your mind. Then you will be able to test and approve what God's will is–his good, pleasing and perfect will." It is your birthright to go after what you want. So claim it and receive it.

Repeat after me:

"I do not allow the conditions that were forced upon me to guide me any longer. It is my life, and I take control of it. I love myself. I am made in the image of the creator. I meditate and pray for my heart's happiest desires. I am grateful for all that I have. I have changed my perspective for the better. I have forgiven the mistakes of myself and others of my past. My faith trumps my fear. I create new successful habits. I workout to keep my mind and body at ease. I believe it so I will achieve it. I am born to prosper. I am a King or Queen."

Now there is only one choice to make, so make sure you choose to...

Be Free!

Notes for Self

Extra Tools For You

ABC Affirmations:
Using each letter of the alphabet, write down a positive adjective that you wish to affirm in your life. Read this daily and believe that no matter what, "this is who I am!"

- I am ______________________________
- I am ______________________________
- I am ______________________________
- I am ______________________________
- I am ______________________________
- I am ______________________________
- I am ______________________________
- I am ______________________________
- I am ______________________________
- I am ______________________________

- I am ________________________________
- I am ________________________________
- I am ________________________________
- I am ________________________________
- I am ________________________________
- I am ________________________________
- I am ________________________________
- I am ________________________________
- I am ________________________________
- I am ________________________________
- I am ________________________________
- I am ________________________________
- I am ________________________________
- I am ________________________________
- I am ________________________________
- I am ________________________________

I am grateful for...

Below list 5 things you are grateful for.

- I am grateful for

- I am grateful for

- I am grateful for

- I am grateful for

- I am grateful for

Creation Zone:

Remember **YOU** are the creator! Below create the life you desire. The life you choose to have *Faith over Fear* in. Use as much detail as possible, express your desired character, relationships, finances, or material items. After writing it down in detail, visualize it, feel it, believe it. Come back to it daily, allow this to be a reminder of the life that you are creating for yourself!

IV

X

Meet The Authors

Deion Pierre

Deion Pierre is a father, social media influencer, and spiritual health and wealth coach. He received a B.S. in Public Health from Samford University in 2017. Using his social media, Deion inspires others through motivation of self-realization and his coaching program *I am Love Everyday.*

Deion is also a co-founder of a podcast *Dream Talk* and Dream Team apparel. While currently obtaining his Holistic Coach Certification with Radiant Health Institute, Deion continues to impact his community through his work and wise words!

Tia Bernice

Tia Bernice is an educator and children's health advocate. She received a B.S. in Psychology from Virginia Commonwealth University in 2016 and has advocated for the well being of children for the last 8 years as an instructor and influencer.

Tia is a children's book creator, co-host of the podcast "DreamTalk," and co-founder of Dream Team Apparels. Tia's brand represents the importance of protecting your mental, physical, and spiritual health, as well as your "Inner-G." Leading with love and light, Tia's greatest motivation is to spread peace and positivity.

Abraham Sculley

Abraham Sculley is a husband, educator, author, fitness trainer, and highly sought-after mental health speaker. He received his B.A. in Psychology from the University of West Florida in 2019 and currently lives in Pensacola, FL with his wife Estefania Sculley and dog, Gypsy.

As the founder of Speaks 2 Inspire, LLC, an organization dedicated to mental health awareness, Abraham has impacted audiences around the United States, including professionals in health care organizations, leaders in for-profit organizations, nationally acclaimed non-profit agencies, and students and professors at major universities and colleges. Abraham continues to follow his passion of assisting others in achieving optimal health holistically.

Evencia Janvier

Evencia Janvier, is an inspirational entrepreneur. She managed to get a bartender's license while maintaining her 9-5 and started a business, Jell-E Shots. It started with just a few events for a friend, but while doing the events she was inspired.

That sparked the push for her to go out on faith and start Jell-E Shots, which has established itself in the South Florida area. Growing from just jell-o shot cups and syringes, Evencia began making drinks, slushies, and much more. Evencia also participates in feeding the homeless and donating to children.

Lerone Gray

Lerone "Roc" Gray is a Performance Coach and founder of Go Hard Performance systems. Go Hard Performance Systems is a strength & performance brand focused on helping people "Grow in Greatness" through a holistic approach to their health.

His focus is to challenge people outside of their norm and most importantly teach them the best ways to move for how they want to live their life.

Jazmin Kylene

Jazmin Kylene is a conscious media journalist and certified spiritual counselor. Guided by her purpose, she created the conscious media platform Lali La Luna TV, seen in over four million homes on all streaming services.

Jazmin has collaborated with outlets like Black Girl In Om and Ethel's Club, led Sacred Healing Circles, designed a line of Color Healing merchandise, and currently provides one-on-one natal chart and tarot readings, spiritual counseling sessions, and reiki healing. She has furthered her studies with the Holistic Arts Institute and Oak Astrology School.

Timone Brown

Timone Brown is a father, husband, coach, speaker and creator. As the founder of Won Up Prep Academy Timone built a coaching company geared to the holistic development of athletes. Timone is also the Vice President of non-profit organization, Blaize'N Awareness Against Drugs (BAAD).

Timone also has 5+ years of inspirational and motivational speaking under his belt. Using his experience and story to uplift and shift the perspective of others he has been blessed to speak in front of various organizations such as St. Joseph's Villa, JMU, Anne Arundel Community College, University of Charleston and the Virginia Department of Corrections.

Referenced Works

Brown, R. P., & Gerbarg, P. L. (2012). The healing power of the breath: Simple techniques to reduce stress and anxiety, enhance concentration, and balance your emotions. Boston, MA: Trumpeter.

Glenn, Jamie. Walk Tall, You're a Daughter of God. Deseret Book Co., 1994.

Henderson, Robert. Spiritual Principles For A Prosperous Life. CreateSpace Independent Publishing Platform , 2012.

Kimbro, Dennis Paul, and Napoleon Hill. Think and Grow Rich: A Black Choice. Fawcett Columbine, 1997.

Ravenola, Dean. "How Playing the Joker Changed Heath Ledger for Good." Looper.com, Looper, 6 May 2020, www.looper.com/141474/how-playing-the-joker-changed-heath-ledger-for-good/.

Roth, R., & Occhiogrosso, P. (1998). The healing path of prayer: A modern mystic's guide to spiritual power. New York: Three Rivers Press.

Terson, Robert. "The Elephant Rope - Author Unknown." Selling Fearlessly, www.sellingfearlessly.com/2014/01/03/the-elephant-rope-author-unknown/.

Made in the USA
Columbia, SC
01 June 2021